COMPACT DISC PAGE AND BAND INFORMATION

MMO CD 3073

Music Minus One

MOZART
Concerto #14 in Eb Major
for Piano and Orchestra
K.449

Band No. Complete Version		Band No. Minus Accmpt.	Page No.
1	1st mvt. Allegro vivace	4	5
2	2nd mvt. Andante	5	26
3	3rd mvt. Allegro ma non troppo	6	36

This concerto, completed on February 9, 1784, was written for Barbara Ployer, a talented young pianist who lived in Vienna. In comparing it with the concertos in B♭, D, and G (K. 450, 451, 453), Mozart wrote: "This is a concerto of a quite special kind, and written more for a small than a large orchestra." The accompaniment is scored for 2 violins, viola, and bass with 2 oboes and 2 horns *ad libitum*.

Music Minus One Piano

3073

W.A. MOZART

Concerto No.14 in Eb Major for Piano and Orchestra

Printed in Canada

W.A.MOZART
Concerto No.14 in Eb Major, K. 449

W.A.Mozart
(1756-1791)

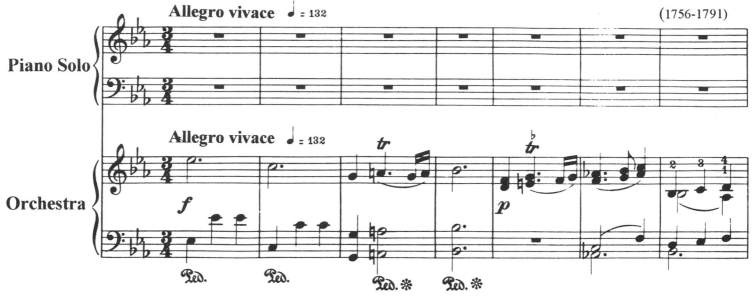

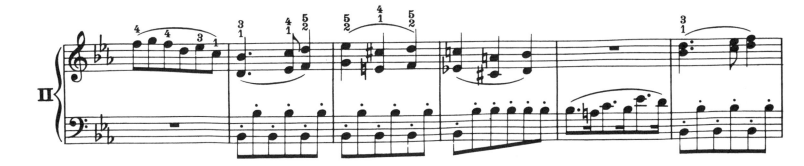

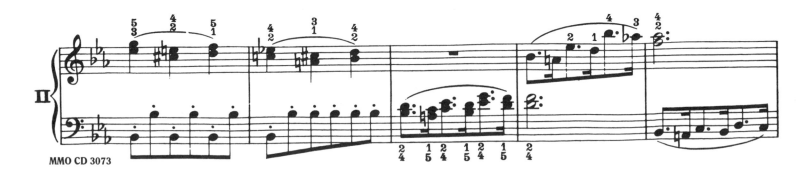

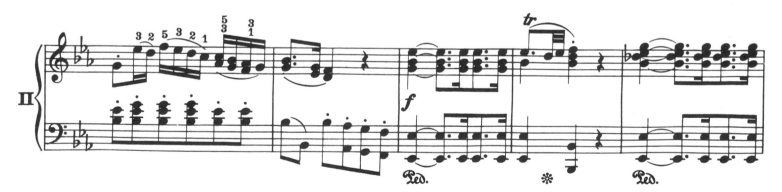

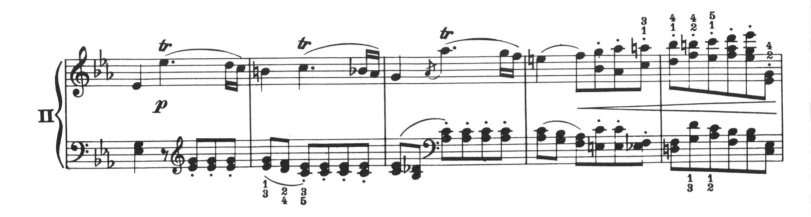

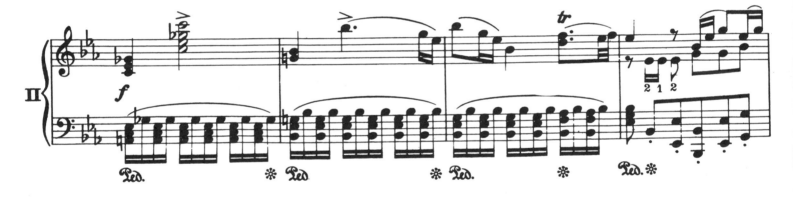

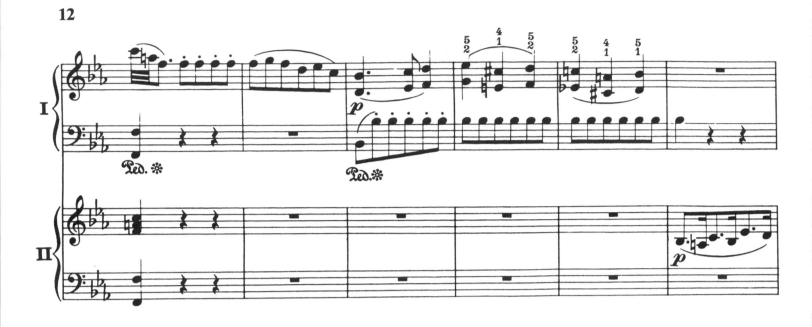

MMO CD 3073

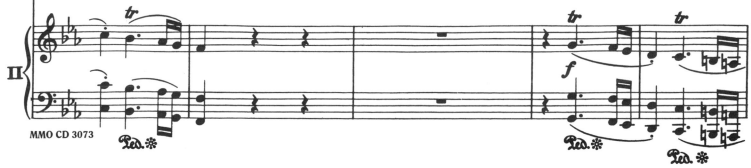

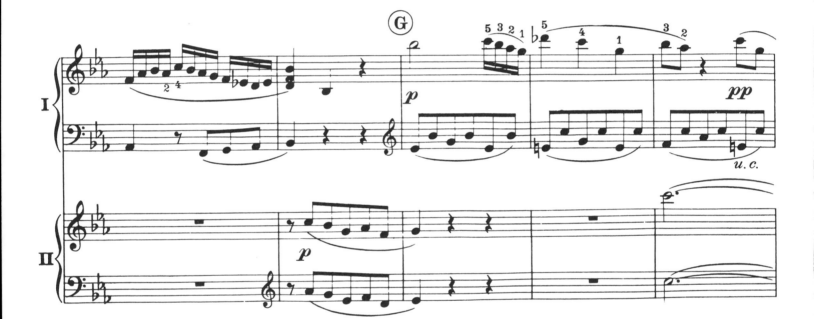

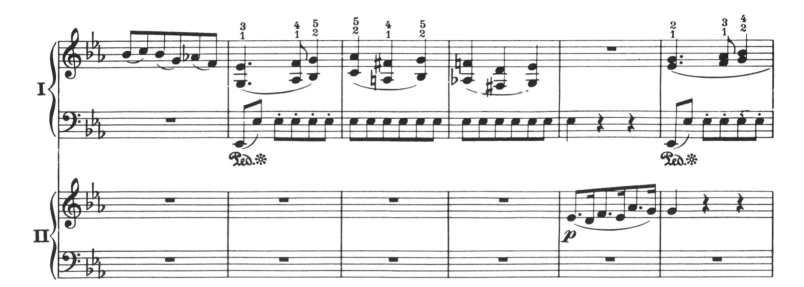

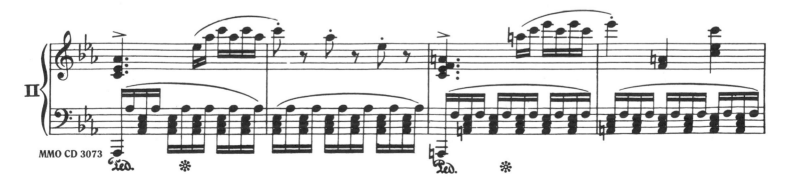

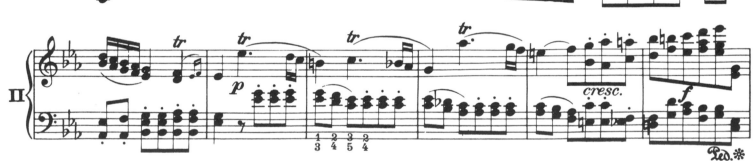

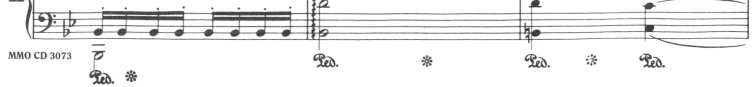

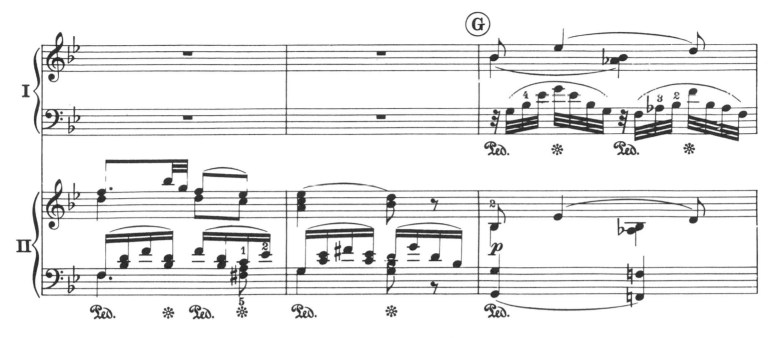

Allegro ma non troppo ♩ = 150

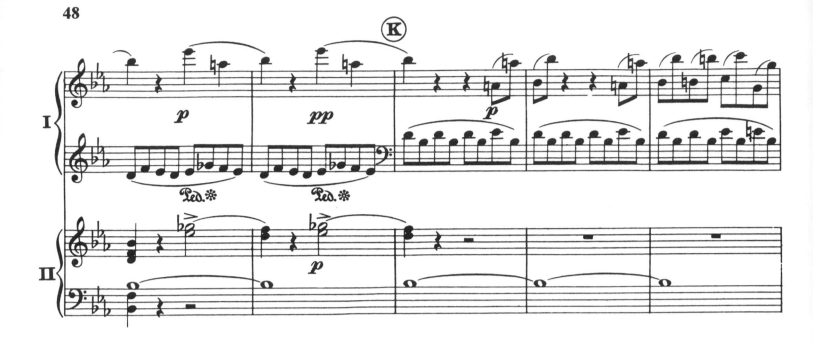

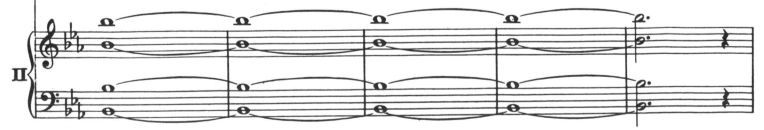

MMO CD 3073

Cadenza

ritard

MMO Compact Disc Catalog

BROADWAY

____ LES MISERABLES/PHANTOM OF THE OPERA ....MMO CD 1016
____ HITS OF ANDREW LLOYD WEBBER ....MMO CD 1054
____ GUYS AND DOLLS ....MMO CD 1067
____ WEST SIDE STORY   2 CD Set ....MMO CD 1100
____ CABARET   2 CD Set ....MMO CD 1110
____ BROADWAY HEROES AND HEROINES ....MMO CD 1121
____ CAMELOT ....MMO CD 1173
____ BEST OF ANDREW LLOYD WEBBER ....MMO CD 1130
____ THE SOUND OF BROADWAY ....MMO CD 1133
____ BROADWAY MELODIES ....MMO CD 1134
____ BARBRA'S BROADWAY ....MMO CD 1144
____ JEKYLL & HYDE ....MMO CD 1151
____ SHOWBOAT ....MMO CD 1160
____ MY FAIR LADY   2 CD Set ....MMO CD 1174
____ OKLAHOMA ....MMO CD 1175
____ THE SOUND OF MUSIC   2 CD Set ....MMO CD 1176
____ SOUTH PACIFIC ....MMO CD 1177
____ THE KING AND I ....MMO CD 1178
____ FIDDLER ON THE ROOF   2 CD Set ....MMO CD 1179
____ CAROUSEL ....MMO CD 1180
____ PORGY AND BESS ....MMO CD 1181
____ THE MUSIC MAN ....MMO CD 1183
____ ANNIE GET YOUR GUN   2 CD Set ....MMO CD 1186
____ HELLO DOLLY!   2 CD Set ....MMO CD 1187
____ OLIVER   2 CD Set ....MMO CD 1189
____ SUNSET BOULEVARD ....MMO CD 1193
____ GREASE ....MMO CD 1196
____ SMOKEY JOE'S CAFE ....MMO CD 1197
____ MISS SAIGON ....MMO CD 1226

CLARINET

____ MOZART CONCERTO, IN A, K.622 ....MMO CD 3201
____ WEBER CONCERTO NO. 1 in Fm. STAMITZ CONC. No. 3 IN Bb ...MMO CD 3202
____ SPOHR CONCERTO NO. 1 in C MINOR OP. 26 ....MMO CD 3203
____ WEBER CONCERTO OP. 26, BEETHOVEN TRIO OP. 11 ....MMO CD 3204
____ FIRST CHAIR CLARINET SOLOS ....MMO CD 3205
____ THE ART OF THE SOLO CLARINET: ....MMO CD 3206
____ MOZART QUINTET IN A, K.581 ....MMO CD 3207
____ BRAHMS SONATAS OP. 120 NO. 1 & 2 ....MMO CD 3208
____ WEBER GRAND DUO CONCERTANT WAGNER ADAGIO ....MMO CD 3209
____ SCHUMANN FANTASY OP. 73, 3 ROMANCES OP. 94 .... MMO CD 3210
____ EASY CLARINET SOLOS Volume 1 - STUDENT LEVEL .... MMO CD 3211
____ EASY CLARINET SOLOS Volume 2 - STUDENT LEVEL .... MMO CD 3212
____ EASY JAZZ DUETS - STUDENT LEVEL .... MMO CD 3213
____ VISIONS The Clarinet Artistry of Ron Odrich .... MMO CD 3214
____ IN A LEAGUE OF HIS OWN Popular Songs played by Ron Odrich and You ....MMO CD 3215
____ SINATRA SET TO MUSIC Kern, Weill, Gershwin, Howard and You ....MMO CD 3216
____ STRAVINSKY: L'HISTOIRE DU SOLDAT ....MMO CD 3217
____ ECLECTIC CLARINET Larry Linkon (2 CD Set) ....MMO CD 3218
____ JAZZ STANDARDS WITH STRINGS FOR CLARINET (2 CD Set) ....MMO CD 3219
____ RON ODRICH PLAYS STANDARDS ....MMO CD 3220
____ BEGINNING CONTEST SOLOS - Jerome Bunke, Clinician .....MMO CD 3221
____ BEGINNING CONTEST SOLOS - Harold Wright ....MMO CD 3222
____ INTERMEDIATE CONTEST SOLOS - Stanley Drucker ....MMO CD 3223
____ INTERMEDIATE CONTEST SOLOS - Jerome Bunke, Clinician .. MMO CD 3224
____ ADVANCED CONTEST SOLOS - Stanley Drucker .... MMO CD 3225
____ ADVANCED CONTEST SOLOS - Harold Wright .... MMO CD 3226
____ INTERMEDIATE CONTEST SOLOS - Stanley Drucker ....MMO CD 3227
____ ADVANCED CONTEST SOLOS - Stanley Drucker .... MMO CD 3228
____ ADVANCED CONTEST SOLOS - Harold Wright .... MMO CD 3229
____ BRAHMS Clarinet Quintet in Bm, Op. 115 ....MMO CD 3230
____ TEACHER'S PARTNER Basic Clarinet Studies ....MMO CD 3231
____ JEWELS FOR WOODWIND QUINTET ....MMO CD 3232
____ WOODWIND QUINTETS minus CLARINET ....MMO CD 3233
____ FROM DIXIE to SWING ....MMO CD 3234
____ BEETHOVEN: QUINTET FOR CLARINET in Eb Major, Opus 16 ..MMO CD 3235
____ MOZART: QUINTET FOR CLARINET in Eb. K.452 ....MMO CD 3236
____ THE VIRTUOSO CLARINETIST Baermann Method, Op. 63 4 CD Set ....MMO CD 3240
____ ART OF THE CLARINET Baermann Method, Op. 64 4 CD Set .....MMO CD 3241
____ POPULAR CONCERT FAVORITES WITH ORCHESTRA ....MMO CD 3242
____ BAND-AIDS CONCERT BAND FAVORITES WITH ORCHESTRA ....MMO CD 3243
____ WORLD FAVORITES Student Editions, 41 Easy Selections (1st-2nd year) ......MMO CD 3244
____ CLASSIC THEMES Student Editions, 27 Easy Songs (2nd-3rd year) ....MMO CD 3245

PIANO

____ BEETHOVEN CONCERTO NO. 1 IN C ....MMO CD 3001
____ BEETHOVEN CONCERTO NO. 2 IN Bb ....MMO CD 3002
____ BEETHOVEN CONCERTO NO. 3 IN C MINOR ....MMO CD 3003

____ BEETHOVEN CONCERTO NO. 4 IN G ....MMO CD 3004
____ BEETHOVEN CONCERTO NO. 5 IN Eb (2 CD SET) ....MMO CD 3005
____ GRIEG CONCERTO IN A MINOR OP.16 ....MMO CD 3006
____ RACHMANINOFF CONCERTO NO. 2 IN C MINOR ....MMO CD 3007
____ SCHUMANN CONCERTO IN A MINOR ....MMO CD 3008
____ BRAHMS CONCERTO NO. 1 IN D MINOR (2 CD SET) ....MMO CD 3009
____ CHOPIN CONCERTO NO. 1 IN E MINOR OP. 11 ....MMO CD 3010
____ MENDELSSOHN CONCERTO NO. 1 IN G MINOR ....MMO CD 3011
____ MOZART CONCERTO NO. 9 IN Eb K.271 ....MMO CD 3012
____ MOZART CONCERTO NO. 12 IN A K.414 ....MMO CD 3013
____ MOZART CONCERTO NO. 20 IN D MINOR K.466 ....MMO CD 3014
____ MOZART CONCERTO NO. 23 IN A K.488 ....MMO CD 3015
____ MOZART CONCERTO NO. 24 IN C MINOR K.491 ....MMO CD 3016
____ MOZART CONCERTO NO. 26 IN D K.537, CORONATION ....MMO CD 3017
____ MOZART CONCERTO NO. 17 IN G K.453 ....MMO CD 3018
____ LISZT CONCERTO NO. 1 IN Eb, WEBER OP. 79 ....MMO CD 3019
____ LISZT CONCERTO NO. 2 IN A, HUNGARIAN FANTASIA ....MMO CD 3020
____ J.S. BACH CONCERTO IN F MINOR, J.C. BACH CON. IN Eb ....MMO CD 3021
____ J.S. BACH CONCERTO IN D MINOR ....MMO CD 3022
____ HAYDN CONCERTO IN D ....MMO CD 3023
____ HEART OF THE PIANO CONCERTO ....MMO CD 3024
____ THEMES FROM GREAT PIANO CONCERTI ....MMO CD 3025
____ TSCHAIKOVSKY CONCERTO NO. 1 IN Bb MINOR ....MMO CD 3026
____ ART OF POPULAR PIANO PLAYING, Vol. 1 STUDENT LEVEL ....MMO CD 3033
____ ART OF POPULAR PIANO PLAYING, Vol. 2 STUDENT LEVEL 2 CD Set....MMO CD 3034
____ 'POP' PIANO FOR STARTERS STUDENT LEVEL ....MMO CD 3035
____ DVORAK TRIO IN A MAJOR, OP. 90 "Dumky Trio" ....MMO CD 3037
____ DVORAK QUINTET IN A MAJOR, OP. 81 ....MMO CD 3038
____ MENDELSSOHN TRIO IN D MAJOR, OP. 49 ....MMO CD 3039
____ MENDELSSOHN TRIO IN C MINOR, OP. 66 ....MMO CD 3040
____ BLUES FUSION FOR PIANO ....MMO CD 3049
____ CLAUDE BOLLING SONATA FOR FLUTE AND JAZZ PIANO TRIO ...MMO CD 3050
____ TWENTY DIXIELAND CLASSICS ....MMO CD 3051
____ TWENTY RHYTHM BACKGROUNDS TO STANDARDS ....MMO CD 3052
____ FROM DIXIE to SWING ....MMO CD 3053
____ J.S. BACH BRANDENBURG CONCERTO NO. 5 IN D MAJOR ....MMO CD 3054
____ BACH Cm CONC. - 2 PIANOS / SCHUMANN & VAR., OP. 46 - 2 PIANOS.......MMO CD 3055
____ J.C. BACH Bm CONC./HAYDN C CONCERT./HANDEL CONC. GROSSO-D ....MMO CD 3056
____ J.S. BACH TRIPLE CONCERTO IN A MINOR ....MMO CD 3057
____ FRANCK SYM. VAR. / MENDELSSOHN: CAPRICCO BRILLANT .....MMO CD 3058
____ C.P.E. BACH CONCERTO IN A MINOR ....MMO CD 3059
____ STRETCHIN' OUT-'Comping' with a Jazz Rhythm Section ...MMO CD 3060
____ RAVEL: PIANO TRIO ....MMO CD 3061
____ THE JIM ODRICH EXPERIENCE Pop Piano Played Easy ....MMO CD 3062
____ POPULAR PIANO MADE EASY Arranged by Jim Odrich ....MMO CD 3063
____ SCHUMANN: Piano Trio in D Minor, Opus 63 ....MMO CD 3064
____ BEETHOVEN: Trio No. 8 & Trio No. 11, "Kakadu" Variations ....MMO CD 3065
____ SCHUBERT: Piano Trio in Bb Major, Opus 99 (2 CD Set) ..MMO CD 3066
____ SCHUBERT: Piano Trio in Eb Major, Opus 100 (2 CD Set) .MMO CD 3067
____ POPULAR SONGS Arranged by Jim Odrich ....MMO CD 3069
____ BEETHOVEN: QUINTET FOR PIANO in Eb Major, Opus 16 .....MMO CD 3070
____ MOZART: QUINTET FOR PIANO in Eb, K.452 ....MMO CD 3071
____ MOZART: PIANO CONCERTO #21 IN C MAJOR, K.467 ....MMO CD 3072
____ MOZART: PIANO CONCERTO KV 449. ....MMO CD 3073

PIANO - FOUR HANDS

____ RACHMANINOFF Six Scenes ....4-5th year ....MMO CD 3027
____ ARENSKY 6 Pieces, STRAVINSKY 3 Easy Dances...2-3rd year ...MMO CD 3028
____ FAURE: The Dolly Suite ....MMO CD 3029
____ DEBUSSY: Four Pieces ....MMO CD 3030
____ SCHUMANN Pictures from the East...........4-5th year ...MMO CD 3031
____ BEETHOVEN Three Marches ....4-5th year ...MMO CD 3032
____ MOZART COMPLETE MUSIC FOR PIANO FOUR HANDS 2 CD Set ...MMO CD 3036
____ MAYKAPAR First Steps, OP. 29..............1-2nd year ...MMO CD 3041
____ TSCHAIKOVSKY: 50 Russian Folk Songs ....MMO CD 3042
____ BIZET: 12 Children's Games ....MMO CD 3043
____ GRETCHANINOFF: ON THE GREEN MEADOW ....MMO CD 3044
____ POZZOLI: SMILES OF CHILDHOOD ....MMO CD 3045
____ DIABELLI: PLEASURES OF YOUTH ....MMO CD 3046
____ SCHUBERT: FANTASIA & GRAND SONATA ....MMO CD 3047

VIOLIN

____ BRUCH CONCERTO NO. 1 IN G MINOR OP.26 ....MMO CD 3100
____ MENDELSSOHN CONCERTO IN E MINOR ....MMO CD 3101
____ TSCHAIKOVSKY CONCERTO IN D OP. 35 ....MMO CD 3102
____ BACH DOUBLE CONCERTO IN D MINOR ....MMO CD 3103
____ BACH CONCERTO IN A MINOR, CONCERTO IN E ....MMO CD 3104
____ BACH BRANDENBURG CONCERTI NOS. 4 & 5 ....MMO CD 3105
____ BACH BRANDENBURG CONCERTO NO. 2, TRIPLE CONCERTO ....MMO CD 3106
____ BACH CONCERTO IN DM, (FROM CONCERTO FOR HARPSICHORD) ...MMO CD 3107

MMO Compact Disc Catalog

____BRAHMS CONCERTO IN D OP. 77 ....MMO CD 3108
____CHAUSSON POEME, SCHUBERT RONDO....MMO CD 3109
____LALO SYMPHONIE ESPAGNOLE ....MMO CD 3110
____MOZART CONCERTO IN D K.218, VIVALDI CON. AM OP.3 NO.6 ....MMO CD 3111
____MOZART CONCERTO IN A K.219....MMO CD 3112
____WIENIAWSKI CON. IN D. SARASATE ZIGEUNERWEISEN ....MMO CD 3113
____VIOTTI CONCERTO NO. 22 IN A MINOR....MMO CD 3114
____BEETHOVEN 2 ROMANCES, SONATA NO. 5 IN F "SPRING SONATA" ....MMO CD 3115
____SAINT-SAENS INTRODUCTION & RONDO,
____MOZART SERENADE K. 204, ADAGIO K.261 ....MMO CD 3116
____BEETHOVEN CONCERTO IN D OP. 61(2 CD SET) ....MMO CD 3117
____THE CONCERTMASTER - Orchestral Excerpts ....MMO CD 3118
____AIR ON A G STRING Favorite Encores with Orchestra Easy Medium....MMO CD 3119
____CONCERT PIECES FOR THE SERIOUS VIOLINIST Easy Medium ....MMO CD 3120
____18TH CENTURY VIOLIN PIECES....MMO CD 3121
____ORCHESTRAL FAVORITES - Volume 1 - Easy Level ....MMO CD 3122
____ORCHESTRAL FAVORITES - Volume 2 - Medium Level ....MMO CD 3123
____ORCHESTRAL FAVORITES - Volume 3 - Med to Difficult Level ....MMO CD 3124
____THE THREE B'S BACH/BEETHOVEN/BRAHMS ....MMO CD 3125
____VIVALDI: VIOLIN CONCERTOS ....MMO CD 3126
____VIVALDI-THE FOUR SEASONS (2 CD Set) ....MMO CD 3127
____VIVALDI Concerto in Eb, Op. 8, No. 5. ALBINONI Concerto in A ....MMO CD 3128
____VIVALDI Concerto in E, Op. 3, No. 12. Concerto in C Op. 8, No.6 "Il Piacere" MMO CD 3129
____SCHUBERT Three Sonatinas ....MMO CD 3130
____HAYDN String Quartet Op. 76 No. 1 ....MMO CD 3131
____HAYDN String Quartet Op. 76 No. 2 ....MMO CD 3132
____HAYDN String Quartet Op. 76 No. 3 "Emperor"....MMO CD 3133
____HAYDN String Quartet Op. 76 No. 4 "Sunrise" ....MMO CD 3134
____HAYDN String Quartet Op. 76 No. 5 ....MMO CD 3135
____HAYDN String Quartet Op. 76 No. 6 ....MMO CD 3136
____BEAUTIFUL MUSIC FOR TWO VIOLINS 1st position, vol. 1 ....MMO CD 3137*
____BEAUTIFUL MUSIC FOR TWO VIOLINS 2nd position, vol. 2 ....MMO CD 3138*
____BEAUTIFUL MUSIC FOR TWO VIOLINS 3rd position, vol. 3 ....MMO CD 3139*
____BEAUTIFUL MUSIC FOR TWO VIOLINS 1st, 2nd, 3rd position, vol. 4 ....MMO CD 3140*

*Lovely folk tunes and selections from the classics, chosen for their melodic beauty and technical value. They have been skillfully transcribed and edited by Samuel Applebaum, one of America's foremost teachers.

____HEART OF THE VIOLIN CONCERTO ....MMO CD 3141
____TEACHER'S PARTNER Basic Violin Studies 1st year....MMO CD 3142
____DVORAK STRING TRIO "Terzetto", OP. 74 2 violins/viola ....MMO CD 3143
____SIBELIUS: Concerto in D minor, Op. 47 ....MMO CD 3144
____THEMES FROM THE MAJOR VIOLIN CONCERTI ....MMO CD 3145
____STRAVINSKY: L'HISTOIRE DU SOLDAT....MMO CD 3146
____RAVEL: PIANO TRIO MINUS VIOLIN ....MMO CD 3147
____GREAT VIOLIN MOMENTS....MMO CD 3148
____RAGTIME STRING QUARTETS The Zinn String Quartet....MMO CD 3151
____SCHUMANN: Piano Trio in D minor, Opus 63....MMO CD 3152
____BEETHOVEN: Trio No. 8 & Trio No. 11, "Kakadu" Variations ....MMO CD 3153
____SCHUBERT: Piano Trio in Bb Major, Opus 99 Minus Violin (2 CD Set) ....MMO CD 3154
____SCHUBERT: Piano Trio in Eb Major, Opus 100 Minus Violin (2 CD Set) ....MMO CD 3155
____BEETHOVEN: STRING QUARTET in A minor, Opus 132 (2 CD Set) ....MMO CD 3156
____DVORAK QUINTET in A major, Opus 81 Minus Violin ....MMO CD 3157
____BEETHOVEN: STRING QTS No. 1 in F major & No. 4 in C minor, Opus 18 ....MMO CD 3158
____HAYDN Three Trios with Piano & Cello....MMO CD 3159
____MOZART: CONCERTO NO. 3 FOR VIOLIN AND ORCHESTRA. ....MMO CD 3160
____MISCHA ELMAN FAVORITE ENCORES....MMO CD 3162
____MISCHA ELMAN CONCERT FAVORITES....MMO CD 3163
____JASCHA HEIFETZ FAVORITE ENCORES. ....MMO CD 3164
____FRITZ KREISLER FAVORITE ENCORES ....MMO CD 3165

GUITAR

____BOCCHERINI Quintet No. 4 in D "Fandango" ....MMO CD 3601
____GIULIANI Quintet in A Op. 65 ....MMO CD 3602
____CLASSICAL GUITAR DUETS ....MMO CD 3603
____RENAISSANCE & BAROQUE GUITAR DUETS....MMO CD 3604
____CLASSICAL & ROMANTIC GUITAR DUETS ....MMO CD 3605
____GUITAR AND FLUTE DUETS Volume 1 ....MMO CD 3606
____GUITAR AND FLUTE DUETS Volume 2 ....MMO CD 3607
____BLUEGRASS GUITAR....MMO CD 3608
____GEORGE BARNES GUITAR METHOD Lessons from a Master ....MMO CD 3609
____HOW TO PLAY FOLK GUITAR 2 CD Set....MMO CD 3610
____FAVORITE FOLKS SONGS FOR GUITAR....MMO CD 3611
____FOR GUITARS ONLY! Jimmy Raney Small Band Arrangements ....MMO CD 3612
____TEN DUETS FOR TWO GUITARS Geo. Barnes/Carl Kress....MMO CD 3613
____PLAY THE BLUES GUITAR A Dick Weissman Method....MMO CD 3614
____ORCHESTRAL GEMS FOR CLASSICAL GUITAR....MMO CD 3615

FLUTE

____MOZART Concerto No. 2 in D, QUANTZ Concerto in G ....MMO CD 3300
____MOZART Concerto in G K.313 ....MMO CD 3301
____BACH Suite No. 2 in B Minor....MMO CD 3302
____BOCCHERINI Concerto in D, VIVALDI Concerto in G Minor "La Notte",
____MOZART Andante for Strings ....MMO CD 3303
____HAYDN Divertimento, VIVALDI Concerto in D Op. 10 No. 3 "Bullfinch",
____FREDERICK THE GREAT Concerto in C ....MMO CD 3304
____VIVALDI Conc. in F; TELEMANN Conc. in D; LECLAIR Conc. in C ....MMO CD 3305
____BACH Brandenburg No. 2 in F, HAYDN Concerto in D ....MMO CD 3306
____BACH Triple Concerto, VIVALDI Concerto in D Minor....MMO CD 3307
____MOZART Quartet in F, STAMITZ Quartet in F....MMO CD 3308
____HAYDN 4 London Trios for 2 Flutes & Cello ....MMO CD 3309
____BACH Brandenburg Concerti Nos. 4 & 5 ....MMO CD 3310
____MOZART 3 Flute Quartets in D, A and C ....MMO CD 3311
____TELEMANN Suite in A Minor, GLUCK Scene from 'Orpheus',
____PERGOLESI Concerto in G (2 CD Set) ....MMO CD 3312
____FLUTE SONG: Easy Familiar Classics ....MMO CD 3313
____VIVALDI Concerti In D, G, and F ....MMO CD 3314
____VIVALDI Concerti in A Minor, G, and D ....MMO CD 3315
____EASY FLUTE SOLOS Beginning Students Volume 1 ....MMO CD 3316
____EASY FLUTE SOLOS Beginning Students Volume 2 ....MMO CD 3317
____EASY JAZZ DUETS Student Level....MMO CD 3318
____FLUTE & GUITAR DUETS Volume 1 ....MMO CD 3319
____FLUTE & GUITAR DUETS Volume 2 ....MMO CD 3320
____BEGINNING CONTEST SOLOS Murray Panitz ....MMO CD 3321
____BEGINNING CONTEST SOLOS Donald Peck ....MMO CD 3322
____INTERMEDIATE CONTEST SOLOS Julius Baker ....MMO CD 3323
____INTERMEDIATE CONTEST SOLOS Donald Peck ....MMO CD 3324
____ADVANCED CONTEST SOLOS Murray Panitz ....MMO CD 3325
____ADVANCED CONTEST SOLOS Julius Baker....MMO CD 3326
____INTERMEDIATE CONTEST SOLOS Donald Peck ....MMO CD 3327
____ADVANCED CONTEST SOLOS Murray Panitz ....MMO CD 3328
____ADVANCED CONTEST SOLOS Julius Baker....MMO CD 3329
____BEGINNING CONTEST SOLOS Doriot Anthony Dwyer ....MMO CD 3330
____INTERMEDIATE CONTEST SOLOS Doriot Anthony Dwyer....MMO CD 3331
____ADVANCED CONTEST SOLOS Doriot Anthony Dwyer ....MMO CD 3332
____FIRST CHAIR SOLOS with Orchestral Accompaniment ....MMO CD 3333
____TEACHER'S PARTNER Basic Flute Studies 1st year....MMO CD 3334
____THE JOY OF WOODWIND MUSIC ....MMO CD 3335
____JEWELS FOR WOODWIND QUINTET....MMO CD 3336
____TELEMANN TRIO IN F/Bb MAJOR/HANDEL SON.#3 IN C MAJOR ....MMO CD 3340
____MARCELLO/TELEMANN/HANDEL SONATAS IN F MAJOR ....MMO CD 3341
____BOLLING: SUITE FOR FLUTE/JAZZ PIANO TRIO ....MMO CD 3342
____HANDEL / TELEMANN SIX SONATAS 2 CD Set ....MMO CD 3343
____BACH SONATA NO. 1 in B MINOR/KUHLAU E MINOR DUET (2 CD set) ....MMO CD 3344
____KUHLAU TRIO in Eb MAJOR/BACH Eb AND A MAJOR SONATA (2 CD set)..MMO CD 3345
____PEPUSCH SONATA IN C / TELEMANN SONATA IN Cm ....MMO CD 3346
____QUANTZ TRIO SONATA IN Cm / BACH GIGUE / ABEL SON. 2 IN F ....MMO CD 3347
____TELEMANN CONCERTO NO. 1 IN D / CORRETTE SONATA IN E MINOR ....MMO CD 3348
____TELEMANN TRIO IN F / Bb MAJOR / HANDEL SON. #3 IN C MAJOR....MMO CD 3349
____MARCELLO / TELEMANN / HANDEL SONATAS IN F MAJOR ....MMO CD 3350
____CONCERT BAND FAVORITES WITH ORCHESTRA ....MMO CD 3351
____BAND-AIDS CONCERT BAND FAVORITES WITH ORCHESTRA ....MMO CD 3352
____UNSUNG HERO George Roberts ....MMO CD 3353
____WORLD FAVORITES Student Editions, 41 Easy Selections (1st-2nd year)....MMO CD 3354
____CLASSIC THEMES Student Editions, 27 Easy Songs (2nd-3rd year) ....MMO CD 3355

RECORDER

____PLAYING THE RECORDER Folk Songs of Many Nations....MMO CD 3337
____LET'S PLAY THE RECORDER Beginning Children's Method ....MMO CD 3338
____YOU CAN PLAY THE RECORDER Beginning Adult Method ....MMO CD 3339

FRENCH HORN

____MOZART: Concerti No. 2 & No. 3 in Eb. K. 417 & 447 ....MMO CD 3501
____BAROQUE BRASS AND BEYOND ....MMO CD 3502
____MUSIC FOR BRASS ENSEMBLE ....MMO CD 3503
____MOZART: Sonatas for Two Horns ....MMO CD 3504
____BEETHOVEN: QUINTET FOR FRENCH HORN in Eb Major, Opus 16 ....MMO CD 3505
____MOZART: QUINTET FOR FRENCH HORN in Eb, K.452 ....MMO CD 3506
____BEGINNING CONTEST SOLOS Mason Jones ....MMO CD 3511
____BEGINNING CONTEST SOLOS Myron Bloom ....MMO CD 3512
____INTERMEDIATE CONTEST SOLOS Dale Clevenger ....MMO CD 3513
____INTERMEDIATE CONTEST SOLOS Mason Jones ....MMO CD 3514
____ADVANCED CONTEST SOLOS Myron Bloom ....MMO CD 3515
____ADVANCED CONTEST SOLOS Dale Clevenger....MMO CD 3516
____INTERMEDIATE CONTEST SOLOS Mason Jones ....MMO CD 3517
____ADVANCED CONTEST SOLOS Myron Bloom ....MMO CD 3518
____INTERMEDIATE CONTEST SOLOS Dale Clevenger....MMO CD 3519
____FRENCH HORN WOODWIND MUSIC ....MMO CD 3520
____MASTERPIECES FOR WOODWIND QUINTET ....MMO CD 3521
____FRENCH HORN UP FRONT BRASS QUINTETS....MMO CD 3522
____HORN OF PLENTY BRASS QUINTETS ....MMO CD 3523
____BAND-AIDS CONCERT BAND FAVORITES WITH ORCHESTRA ....MMO CD 3524

MMO Compact Disc Catalog

TRUMPET

THREE CONCERTI: HAYDN, TELEMANN, FASCH	MMO CD 3801
TRUMPET SOLOS Student Level Volume 1	MMO CD 3802
TRUMPET SOLOS Student Level Volume 2	MMO CD 3803
EASY JAZZ DUETS Student Level	MMO CD 3804
MUSIC FOR BRASS ENSEMBLE Brass Quintets	MMO CD 3805
FIRST CHAIR TRUMPET SOLOS with Orchestral Accompaniment	MMO CD 3806
THE ART OF THE SOLO TRUMPET with Orchestral Accompaniment	MMO CD 3807
BAROQUE BRASS AND BEYOND Brass Quintets	MMO CD 3808
THE COMPLETE ARBAN DUETS all of the classic studies	MMO CD 3809
SOUSA MARCHES PLUS BEETHOVEN, BERLIOZ, STRAUSS	MMO CD 3810
BEGINNING CONTEST SOLOS Gerard Schwarz	MMO CD 3811
BEGINNING CONTEST SOLOS Armando Ghitalla	MMO CD 3812
INTERMEDIATE CONTEST SOLOS Robert Nagel, Soloist	MMO CD 3813
INTERMEDIATE CONTEST SOLOS Gerard Schwarz	MMO CD 3814
ADVANCED CONTEST SOLOS Robert Nagel, Soloist	MMO CD 3815
CONTEST SOLOS Armando Ghitalla	MMO CD 3816
INTERMEDIATE CONTEST SOLOS Gerard Schwarz	MMO CD 3817
ADVANCED CONTEST SOLOS Robert Nagel, Soloist	MMO CD 3818
ADVANCED CONTEST SOLOS Armando Ghilalla	MMO CD 3819
BEGINNING CONTEST SOLOS Raymond Crisara	MMO CD 3820
BEGINNING CONTEST SOLOS Raymond Crisara	MMO CD 3821
INTERMEDIATE CONTEST SOLOS Raymond Crisara	MMO CD 3822
TEACHER'S PARTNER Basic Trumpet Studies 1st year	MMO CD 3823
TWENTY DIXIELAND CLASSICS	MMO CD 3824
TWENTY RHYTHM BACKGROUNDS TO STANDARDS	MMO CD 3825
FROM DIXIE TO SWING	MMO CD 3826
TRUMPET PIECES BRASS QUINTETS	MMO CD 3827
MODERN BRASS QUINTETS	MMO CD 3828
WHEN JAZZ WAS YOUNG The Bob Wilber All Stars	MMO CD 3829
CLASSIC TRUMPET SELECTIONS WITH PIANO	MMO CD 3830
CONCERT BAND FAVORITES WITH ORCHESTRA	MMO CD 3831
BAND-AIDS CONCERT BAND FAVORITES WITH ORCHESTRA	MMO CD 3832
BRASS TRAX The Trumpet Artistry Of David O'Neill	MMO CD 3833
TRUMPET TRIUMPHANT The Further Adventures Of David O'Neill	MMO CD 3834
WORLD FAVORITES Student Editions, 41 Easy Selections (1st-2nd year)	MMO CD 3836
CLASSIC THEMES Student Editions, 27 Easy Songs (2nd-3rd year)	MMO CD 3837
STRAVINSKY: L'HISTOIRE DU SOLDAT	MMO CD 3835
12 CLASSIC JAZZ STANDARDS Bb/Eb/Bass Clef	MMO CD 7010
12 MORE CLASSIC JAZZ STANDARDS Bb/Eb/Bass Clef	MMO CD 7011

TROMBONE

TROMBONE SOLOS Student Level Volume 1	MMO CD 3901
TROMBONE SOLOS Student Level Volume 2	MMO CD 3902
EASY JAZZ DUETS Student Level	MMO CD 3903
BAROQUE BRASS & BEYOND Brass Quintets	MMO CD 3904
MUSIC FOR BRASS ENSEMBLE Brass Quintets	MMO CD 3905
UNSUNG HERO George Roberts	MMO CD 3906
BIG BAND BALLADS George Roberts	MMO CD 3907
STRAVINSKY: L'HISTOIRE DU SOLDAT	MMO CD 3908
CLASSICAL TROMBONE SOLOS	MMO CD 3909
JAZZ STANDARDS WITH STRINGS (2 CD Set)	MMO CD 3910
BEGINNING CONTEST SOLOS Per Brevig	MMO CD 3911
BEGINNING CONTEST SOLOS Jay Friedman	MMO CD 3912
INTERMEDIATE CONTEST SOLOS Keith Brown, Professor, Indiana U.	MMO CD 3913
INTERMEDIATE CONTEST SOLOS Jay Friedman	MMO CD 3914
ADVANCED CONTEST SOLOS Keith Brown, Professor, Indiana University	MMO CD 3915
ADVANCED CONTEST SOLOS Per Brevig	MMO CD 3916
ADVANCED CONTEST SOLOS Keith Brown, Professor, Indiana University	MMO CD 3917
ADVANCED CONTEST SOLOS Jay Friedman	MMO CD 3918
ADVANCED CONTEST SOLOS Per Brevig	MMO CD 3919
TEACHER'S PARTNER Basic Trombone Studies 1st year	MMO CD 3920
TWENTY DIXIELAND CLASSICS	MMO CD 3924
TWENTY RHYTHM BACKGROUNDS TO STANDARDS	MMO CD 3925
FROM DIXIE TO SWING	MMO CD 3926
STICKS & BONES BRASS QUINTETS	MMO CD 3927
FOR TROMBONES ONLY MORE BRASS QUINTETS	MMO CD 3928
POPULAR CONCERT FAVORITES The Stuttgart Festival Band	MMO CD 3929
BAND-AIDS CONCERT BAND FAVORITES WITH ORCHESTRA	MMO CD 3930
WORLD FAVORITES Student Editions, 41 Easy Selections (1st-2nd year)	MMO CD 3931
CLASSIC THEMES Student Editions, 27 Easy Songs (2nd-3rd year)	MMO CD 3932
12 CLASSIC JAZZ STANDARDS Bb/Eb/Bass Clef	MMO CD 7010
12 MORE CLASSIC JAZZ STANDARDS Bb/Eb/Bass Clef	MMO CD 7011

TENOR SAXOPHONE

TENOR SAXOPHONE SOLOS Student Edition Volume 1	MMO CD 4201
TENOR SAXOPHONE SOLOS Student Edition Volume 2	MMO CD 4202
EASY JAZZ DUETS FOR TENOR SAXOPHONE	MMO CD 4203
FOR SAXES ONLY Arranged by Bob Wilber	MMO CD 4204
BLUES FUSION FOR SAXOPHONE	MMO CD 4205
JOBIM BRAZILIAN BOSSA NOVAS with STRINGS	MMO CD 4206
TWENTY DIXIE CLASSICS	MMO CD 4207
TWENTY RHYTHM BACKGROUNDS TO STANDARDS	MMO CD 4208
PLAY LEAD IN A SAX SECTION	MMO CD 4209
DAYS OF WINE & ROSES Sax Section Minus You	MMO CD 4210
FRENCH & AMERICAN SAXOPHONE QUARTETS	MMO CD 4211
CONCERT BAND FAVORITES WITH ORCHESTRA	MMO CD 4212
BAND AIDS CONCERT BAND FAVORITES	MMO CD 4213
JAZZ JAM FOR TENOR (2 CD Set)	MMO CD 4214
12 CLASSIC JAZZ STANDARDS Bb/Eb/Bass Clef	MMO CD 7010
12 MORE CLASSIC JAZZ STANDARDS Bb/Eb/Bass Clef	MMO CD 7011

CELLO

DVORAK Concerto in B Minor Op. 104 (2 CD Set)	MMO CD 3701
C.P.E. BACH Concerto in A Minor	MMO CD 3702
BOCCHERINI Concerto in Bb, BRUCH Kol Nidrei	MMO CD 3703
TEN PIECES FOR CELLO	MMO CD 3704
SCHUMANN Concerto in Am & Other Selections	MMO CD 3705
CLAUDE BOLLING Suite For Cello & Jazz Piano Trio	MMO CD 3706
RAVEL: PIANO TRIO MINUS CELLO	MMO CD 3707
RAGTIME STRING QUARTETS	MMO CD 3708
SCHUMANN: Piano Trio in D Minor, Opus 63	MMO CD 3709
BEETHOVEN: Piano Trio For Cello	MMO CD 3710
SCHUBERT: Piano Trio in Bb Major, Opus 99 Minus Cello (2 CD Set)	MMO CD 3711
SCHUBERT: Piano Trio in Eb Major, Opus 100 Minus Cello (2 CD Set)	MMO CD 3712
BEETHOVEN: STRING QUARTET in A minor, Opus 132 (2 CD Set)	MMO CD 3713
DVORAK QUINTET in A Major, Opus 81 Minus Cello	MMO CD 3714
BEETHOVEN: SONATA IN A MAJOR, OP. 69 Minus Cello	MMO CD 3715
WINER: Concerto/SCHUBERT: Ave Maria/SAINT-SAENS: Allegro Appass.	MMO CD 3716

OBOE

ALBINONI Concerti in Bb, Op. 7 No. 3, No. 6, D. Op. 9 No. 2 in Dm	MMO CD 3400
TELEMANN Conc. in Fm; HANDEL Conc. in Bb; VIVALDI Conc.in Dm	MMO CD 3401
MOZART Quartet in F K.370, STAMITZ Quartet in F Op. 8 No. 3	MMO CD 3402
BACH Brandenburg Concerto No. 2, Telemann Con. in Am	MMO CD 3403
CLASSIC SOLOS FOR OBOE Delia Montenegro, Soloist	MMO CD 3404
MASTERPIECES FOR WOODWIND QUINTET	MMO CD 3405
THE JOY OF WOODWIND QUINTETS	MMO CD 3406
PEPUSCH SONATAS IN C/TELEMANN SONATA IN Cm	MMO CD 3407
QUANTZ TRIO SONATA IN Cm/BACH GIGUE/ABEL SONATAS IN F	MMO CD 3408
BEETHOVEN: QUINTET FOR OBOE in Eb, Opus 16	MMO CD 3409

ALTO SAXOPHONE

ALTO SAXOPHONE SOLOS Student Edition Volume 1	MMO CD 4101
ALTO SAXOPHONE SOLOS Student Edition Volume 2.	MMO CD 4102
EASY JAZZ DUETS FOR ALTO SAXOPHONE	MMO CD 4103
FOR SAXES ONLY Arranged Bob Wilber	MMO CD 4104
JOBIM BRAZILIAN BOSSA NOVAS with STRINGS	MMO CD 4106
UNSUNG HEROES FOR ALTO SAXOPHONE	MMO CD 4107
BEGINNING CONTEST SOLOS Paul Brodie, Canadian Soloist	MMO CD 4111
BEGINNING CONTEST SOLOS Vincent Abato	MMO CD 4112
INTERMEDIATE CONTEST SOLOS Paul Brodie, Canadian Soloist	MMO CD 4113
INTERMEDIATE CONTEST SOLOS Vincent Abato	MMO CD 4114
ADVANCED CONTEST SOLOS Paul Brodie. Canadian Soloist	MMO CD 4115
ADVANCED CONTEST SOLOS Vincent Abato	MMO CD 4116
ADVANCED CONTEST SOLOS Paul Brodie, Canadian Soloist	MMO CD 4117
Basic Studies for Alto Sax TEACHER'S PARTNER 1st year level	MMO CD 4119
ADVANCED CONTEST SOLOS Vincent Abato	MMO CD 4118
PLAY LEAD IN A SAX SECTION	MMO CD 4120
DAYS OF WINE & ROSES/SENSUAL SAX	MMO CD 4121
TWENTY DIXIELAND CLASSICS	MMO CD 4124
TWENTY RHYTHM BACKGROUNDS TO STANDARDS	MMO CD 4125
CONCERT BAND FAVORITES WITH ORCHESTRA	MMO CD 4126
BAND AIDS CONCERT BAND FAVORITES	MMO CD 4127
MUSIC FOR SAXOPHONE QUARTET	MMO CD 4128
WORLD FAVORITES Student Editions, 41 Easy Selections (1st-2nd year)	MMO CD 4129
CLASSIC THEMES Student Editions, 27 Easy Songs (2nd-3rd year)	MMO CD 4130
12 CLASSIC JAZZ STANDARDS Bb/Eb/Bass Clef	MMO CD 7010
12 MORE CLASSIC JAZZ STANDARDS Bb/Eb/Bass Clef	MMO CD 7011

SOPRANO SAXOPHONE

FRENCH & AMERICAN SAXOPHONE QUARTETS	MMO CD 4801
12 CLASSIC JAZZ STANDARDS Bb/Eb/Bass Clef	MMO CD 7010
12 MORE CLASSIC JAZZ STANDARDS Bb/Eb/Bass Clef	MMO CD 7011

MMO Compact Disc Catalog

BARITONE SAXOPHONE

____ MUSIC FOR SAXOPHONE QUARTET ....MMO CD 4901
____ 12 CLASSIC JAZZ STANDARDS Bb/Eb/Bass Clef ....MMO CD 7010
____ 12 MORE CLASSIC JAZZ STANDARDS Bb/Eb/Bass Clef ....MMO CD 7011

VOCAL

____ SCHUBERT GERMAN LIEDER - High Voice, Volume 1 ....MMO CD 4001
____ SCHUBERT GERMAN LIEDER - Low Voice, Volume 1 ....MMO CD 4002
____ SCHUBERT GERMAN LIEDER - High Voice, Volume 2 ....MMO CD 4003
____ SCHUBERT GERMAN LIEDER - Low Voice, Volume 2 ....MMO CD 4004
____ BRAHMS GERMAN LIEDER - High Voice ....MMO CD 4005
____ BRAHMS GERMAN LIEDER - Low Voice ....MMO CD 4006
____ EVERYBODY'S FAVORITE SONGS - High Voice, Volume 1 ....MMO CD 4007
____ EVERYBODY'S FAVORITE SONGS - Low Voice, Volume 1 ....MMO CD 4008
____ EVERYBODY'S FAVORITE SONGS - High Voice, Volume 2 ....MMO CD 4009
____ EVERYBODY'S FAVORITE SONGS - Low Voice, Volume 2 ....MMO CD 4010
____ 17th/18th CENT. ITALIAN SONGS - High Voice, Volume 1 ....MMO CD 4011
____ 17th/18th CENT. ITALIAN SONGS - Low Voice, Volume 1 ....MMO CD 4012
____ 17th/18th CENT. ITALIAN SONGS - High Voice, Volume 2 ....MMO CD 4013
____ 17th/18th CENT. ITALIAN SONGS - Low Voice, Volume 2 ....MMO CD 4014
____ FAMOUS SOPRANO ARIAS ....MMO CD 4015
____ FAMOUS MEZZO-SOPRANO ARIAS ....MMO CD 4016
____ FAMOUS TENOR ARIAS ....MMO CD 4017
____ FAMOUS BARITONE ARIAS ....MMO CD 4018
____ FAMOUS BASS ARIAS ....MMO CD 4019
____ WOLF GERMAN LIEDER FOR HIGH VOICE ....MMO CD 4020
____ WOLF GERMAN LIEDER FOR LOW VOICE ....MMO CD 4021
____ STRAUSS GERMAN LIEDER FOR HIGH VOICE ....MMO CD 4022
____ STRAUSS GERMAN LIEDER FOR LOW VOICE ....MMO CD 4023
____ SCHUMANN GERMAN LIEDER FOR HIGH VOICE ....MMO CD 4024
____ SCHUMANN GERMAN LIEDER FOR LOW VOICE ....MMO CD 4025
____ MOZART ARIAS FOR SOPRANO ....MMO CD 4026
____ VERDI ARIAS FOR SOPRANO ....MMO CD 4027
____ ITALIAN ARIAS FOR SOPRANO ....MMO CD 4028
____ FRENCH ARIAS FOR SOPRANO ....MMO CD 4029
____ ORATORIO ARIAS FOR SOPRANO ....MMO CD 4030
____ ORATORIO ARIAS FOR ALTO ....MMO CD 4031
____ ORATORIO ARIAS FOR TENOR ....MMO CD 4032
____ ORATORIO ARIAS FOR BASS ....MMO CD 4033
____ BEGINNING SOPRANO SOLOS Kate Hurney ....MMO CD 4041
____ INTERMEDIATE SOPRANO SOLOS Kate Hurney ....MMO CD 4042
____ BEGINNING MEZZO SOPRANO SOLOS Fay Kittelson ....MMO CD 4043
____ INTERMEDIATE MEZZO SOPRANO SOLOS Fay Kittelson ....MMO CD 4044
____ ADVANCED MEZZO SOPRANO SOLOS Fay Kittelson ....MMO CD 4045
____ BEGINNING CONTRALTO SOLOS Carline Ray ....MMO CD 4046
____ BEGINNING TENOR SOLOS George Shirley ....MMO CD 4047
____ INTERMEDIATE TENOR SOLOS George Shirley ....MMO CD 4048
____ ADVANCED TENOR SOLOS George Shirley ....MMO CD 4049
____ TWELVE CLASSIC VOCAL STANDARDS, VOL.1 ....MMO CD 4050
____ TWELVE CLASSIC VOCAL STANDARDS, VOL.2 ....MMO CD 4051
____ SOPRANO ARIAS WITH ORCHESTRA The Viidin Philharmonic Orch. ...MMO CD 4052
____ PUCCINI ARIAS FOR SOPRANO WITH ORCHESTRA ....MMO CD 4053
____ SOPRANO ARIAS WITH ORCHESTRA The Sofia Festival Orch. ....MMO CD 4054
____ VERDI ARIAS FOR MEZZO-SOPRANO WITH ORCHESTRA ....MMO CD 4055
____ BASS-BARITONE ARIAS WITH ORCHESTRA. ....MMO CD 4056
____ TENOR OPERA ARIAS WITH ORCHESTRA ....MMO CD 4057
____ SOPRANO OPERA ARIAS WITH ORCHESTRA ....MMO CD 4058

DOUBLE BASS

____ BEGINNING TO INTERMEDIATE CONTEST SOLOS David Walter ....MMO CD 4301
____ INTERMEDIATE TO ADVANCED CONTEST SOLOS David Walter ....MMO CD 4302
____ FOR BASSISTS ONLY Ken Smith, Soloist ....MMO CD 4303
____ THE BEAT GOES ON Jazz - Funk, Latin, Pop-Rock.....................MMO CD 4304
____ FROM DIXIE TO SWING ....MMO CD 4305
____ STRAVINSKY: L'HISTOIRE DU SOLDAT ....MMO CD 4306

DRUMS

____ MODERN JAZZ DRUMMING 2 CD Set ....MMO CD 5001
____ FOR DRUMMERS ONLY..MMO CD 5002
____ WIPE OUT ....MMO CD 5003
____ SIT-IN WITH JIM CHAPIN ....MMO CD 5004
____ DRUM STAR Trios/Quartets/Quintets Minus You ....MMO CD 5005
____ DRUMPADSTICKSKIN Jazz play-alongs with small groups ....MMO CD 5006
____ JUMP & SWING DRUMS...MMO CD 5007
____ CLASSICAL PERCUSSION 2 CD Set ....MMO CD 5009
____ EIGHT MEN IN SEARCH OF A DRUMMER ....MMO CD 5010

____ FROM DIXIE TO SWING ....MMO CD 5011
____ FABULOUS SOUNDS OF ROCK DRUMS ....MMO CD 5012
____ OPEN SESSION WITH THE GREG BURROWS QUINTET (2 CD Set) ....MMO CD 5013
____ STRAVINSKY: L'HISTOIRE DU SOLDAT ....MMO CD 5014

VIOLA

____ VIOLA SOLOS with piano accompaniment ....MMO CD 4501
____ DVORAK STRING TRIO "Terzetto", OP. 74 2 Vins/Viola ....MMO CD 4502
____ BEETHOVEN: STRING QUARTET in A minor, Opus 132 (2 CD Set) .....MMO CD 4503
____ DVORAK QUINTET in A major, Opus 81 Minus Viola ....MMO CD 4504
____ VIOLA CONCERTI WITH ORCHESTRA J.C. Bach/j\Hofmaister ....MMO CD 4505

VIBES

____ FOR VIBISTS ONLY ....MMO CD 5101
____ GOOD VIB-RATIONS ....MMO CD 5102

BASSOON

____ SOLOS FOR THE BASSOON   Janet Grice, Soloist ....MMO CD 4601
____ MASTERPIECES FOR WOODWIND MUSIC ....MMO CD 4602
____ THE JOY OF WOODWIND QUINTETS ....MMO CD 4603
____ STRAVINSKY: L'HISTOIRE DU SOLDAT ....MMO CD 4604
____ BEETHOVEN: QUINTET FOR BASSOON in Eb, Opus 16 ....MMO CD 4605
____ MOZART: QUINTET FOR BASSOON in Eb, K.452 ....MMO CD 4606

BANJO

____ BLUEGRASS BANJO Classic & Favorite Banjo Pieces ....MMO CD 4401
____ PLAY THE FIVE STRING BANJO Vol. 1 Dick Weissman Method ....MMO CD 4402
____ PLAY THE FIVE STRING BANJO Vol. 2 Dick Weissman Method ....MMO CD 4403

TUBA or BASS TROMBONE

____ HE'S NOT HEAVY, HE'S MY TUBA ....MMO CD 4701
____ SWEETS FOR BRASS ....MMO CD 4702
____ MUSIC FOR BRASS ENSEMBLE ....MMO CD 4703

INSTRUCTIONAL METHODS

____ RUTGERS UNIVERSITY MUSIC DICTATION/EAR TRAINING (7 CD Set) ....MMO CD 7001
____ EVOLUTION OF THE BLUES ....MMO CD 7004
____ THE ART OF IMPROVISATION, VOL. 1 ....MMO CD 7005
____ THE ART OF IMPROVISATION, VOL. 2 ....MMO CD 7006
____ THE BLUES MINUS YOU   Ed Xiques, Soloist ....MMO CD 7007
____ TAKE A CHORUS minus Bb/Eb Instruments..............................MMO CD 7008
____ UNDERSTANDING JAZZ ....MMO CD 7009
____ 12 CLASSIC JAZZ STANDARDS Bb/Eb/Bass Clef..........................MMO CD 7010
____ 12 MORE CLASSIC JAZZ STANDARDS Bb/Eb/Bass Clef ....MMO CD 7011

MMO Music Group • 50 Executive Boulevard, Elmsford, New York 10523, 1-(800) 669-7464
Website: www. minusone.com • E-mail: mmomus@aol.com